WHO'S LOVING YOU?

NATOSHA WALDEN

www.TrueVinePublishing.org

Who's Loving You?
Natosha Walden

Published by
True Vine Publishing Co.
810 Dominican Dr.
Nashville, TN 37228
www.TrueVinePublishing.org

Copyright © 2026 by Natosha Walden

ISBN: 978-1-968092-70-2 Paperback
ISBN: 978-1-968092-71-9 eBook

All rights reserved. No part of this book may be reproduced in any form or by any electronic or mechanical means, including information storage and retrieval systems, without permission in writing from the publisher, except by a reviewer who may quote brief passages in a review.

Printed in the United States of America—First printing.

Unless otherwise indicated, all Scripture quotations are taken from various Bible translations including KJV, NKJV, NIV, AMP, TPT, NLT, and others. Some passages have been paraphrased for clarity, emphasis, and devotional application.

Scripture: Gen 13:8 – Gracious Love

A passage that sums up something. This scripture appears to bring a solution to a problem. You see, both Abram and Lot were well-endowed with both cattle and servants. They both had resources and workers to tend to them. There was a problem that existed between their teams. We don't know how long the problem had been there, we don't know what started it. We do know that there were two mindsets, two opinions, two bosses, and they were now in opposition about one land.

Abram, Lot's Uncle, did not want for there to be bad blood between the two of them, so he suggested a separation. He gave Lot the choice of the lands. Lot chose the land that had the better appearance and that would appear to be the best. Abram blessed him and released him. The story doesn't start here, nor does it end here. God had given specific instructions to Abram about his journey, not Lot.

Abram's heart was to keep and protect his nephew. They came out of Haran together, but did not walk in the same way before GOD.

What do you hear from this scripture? What is God saying to you?

There are many that you may have come out of a place with, but your journey is not the same and you may well need to separate, so that each one can be sensitive to HIS Voice and learn to obey it. Each person must learn to tune into The Voice of Our Father.

There may be times when we will need to come back and help each other later, but stay focused on the call on your life.

Reflection/Your Story:

I, like Abram, was called by GOD to leave the small town that I had grown up in. At first, I didn't know it was to serve GOD because I didn't intimately know HIM yet. During the journey, I encountered The Most High GOD and HE changed me. Others from my past wanted to come and see what had happened in my life because they were in need. I constantly brought others along, and many times came to a place where it was time to part. That is every believer's life. Today, I am still learning to listen and know where, when, and who goes with you. Follow HIS Voice, not your kindness ❤

Activity:

Sit down and write out a chapter of your life. List all of the players in your chapter. How do they help your story? How do they hinder your story? Ask GOD what part they are really supposed to play in your story. Then, allow GOD to rewrite your story.

Prayer:

Father, just as you called Abram to leave a place and follow You, we Your children are also to leave the places You call us out of. May we believe You and know that You will account it to us as righteousness.

May we submit to Your process for our lives. May we know what YOUR good and perfect Will is for our lives, and may we pursue it with great passion. We love You and we need

You. Thank You Lord for the leadership of Your Holy Spirit, to keep us in the truth. Yours is the kingdom and the power and the glory forever. In Jesus Name, Amen.

Scripture: Gen. 13:8 - Gracious Love

What do you hear from this scripture? What is God saying to you?

Reflection/Your Story:

Activity:

Questions to Ponder:

Prayer:

Scripture: 1 Sam. 20:17 – Love for Others

Jonathan caused David to swear again, because he loved him; for he loved him as he loved his own soul.

What do you hear from this scripture? What is God saying to you?

A different kind of friendship exists here. This relationship is a rare find. This is specifically connected to some of my ministry relationships

Reflection/Your Story:

As I perceive such matters, few relationships like David and Jonathan exist. This is a sacred exchange. Maybe due to the amount of investment, little is known about how to obtain and maintain a covenant relationship like theirs. I am grateful that the all-wise God gave us such a standard for intimate, platonic friendships. While marriage is a sacrament, a Christ-centered covenant friendship could be an advantageous precursor to living holy. It was simple to understand why marriage is covenant because of the implied permanency and the invitation of Christ's habitation in us. A prophetic process teaching for his return is needed.

This verse is held reverently because of Jonathan's insistence on the vow. The request evokes such sacrifice. Even in a friendship today, the weight of a king's reign and royal family obligations would suggest that any potential king would do well to be reserved about who connects with him. When this heir is vulnerable with his heart and his future, you know you're getting a clue to where a hidden key to an eternal door is tucked away. I think of pop culture and the breaking news of Prince Harry and Meghan Markel's engagement, marriage and the departure from England's royal family. Although I don't know anything about them intimately, I was intrigued by the decision of the Duke and Duchess of Sussex. Covenant will change the heart of a prince.

The way our up close and personal GOD cultivates circumstances that could produce such a sacred connection is worthy of contemplation. It is unique in that it is the only friendship in scripture esteemed in this manner. The exemplary actions of these two monarchs makes our strive toward kingdom living less of a legality by checking boxes off our list of law and more living love loudly and present.

Activity:

Text some of your close friends and ask them their thoughts on this verse.

Be bold enough to ask if this might describe any friendships that they are privy to.

Questions to Ponder:

1. How can we "deal kindly" in our beloved circles of influence?
2. Can we be vulnerable enough to extend ourselves to covenant friends by offering, "Whatever you say, I will do for you"?

Prayer:

"Remember not the former things; neither consider the things of old. Behold, I will do a new thing; now it shall spring forth; shall ye not know it? I will even make a way in the wilderness and rivers in the desert" (Isaiah 43:18-19).

Scripture: Gen 13:8 -Gracious Love

What do you hear from this scripture? What is God saying to you?

Reflection/Your Story:

Activity:

____

____

____

____

____

Questions to Ponder:

____

____

____

____

____

Prayer:

____

____

____

____

____

Scripture: Zephaniah 3:9 – Purifying Love

Then l will purify the speech of all people, so that everyone can worship the LORD together. In the end I will turn things around for the people.

For then will I turn to the people a pure language that they may all call upon the name of the LORD and serve Him with one consent (shoulder to shoulder).

What do you hear from this scripture? What is GOD saying to you?

What I hear from this scripture

It's saying that there is no language barriers when it comes to the LORD and His WORD; just like when the Holy Spirit fell down at Pentecost; and what GOD is saying to me is that my words have power, so what am I saying and what effect are they having on those I come in contact with?

Reflection: 1 Peter 1:22 teaches that by obeying the truth, you have sincere love for each other; so I must first believe the words I'm releasing. I must have courage, character, and wisdom to speak the truth; and pray, have faith, and use my actions in line with the words I release.

GOD's purifying love gives us a new identity; we are children of GOD.

Gives us promise for the future; the best is yet to come.

Gives us motivation; faith with shoes on.

My Story: My name is Patricia and I love the Lord, not because of what He's done, but because of who He is. He has changed my language and outlook on life. I've always prayed, but had never connected my words and actions to my prayers until I heard the Lord speak to me. I had broken my ankle and was told that it would not heal, and my right lower leg would have to be amputated, so I prayed not my words, but His words, and in the midst of praying, I heard the Lord ask me if I believed what I was saying and praying. He then said prove it, for words without actions are meaningless. I was praising and worshipping and heard a song by Byron Cage called "Broken But I'm Healed." This song was talking about me and it ministered to me. I went to church and told my Pastor and explained what had happened and told her that I needed to dance for my healing; mind you, I was in a cast up to my knee. From that day forth, I have been changed; my language is not the same, and neither am I.

Questions to Ponder:

The song says: I have a message for you today that when you leave here, you won't be the same, so go tell the world, what you have received.

Prayer:

Heavenly Father, I come to you asking you to change me Lord, my language, my life, and my ways. May they be of You. Help me to be a light in darkness. So that when people encounter me they meet You. May my words ignite a fire in them, causing them to want You, Your righteousness, and Your kingdom. May it change their language to a purified love. For blessed are the pure in heart, for they shall see God. I ask this in Jesus's name. Amen.

Scripture: Gen 13:8 -Gracious Love

What do you hear from this scripture? What is God saying to you?

Reflection/Your Story:

Activity:

____

Questions to Ponder:

Prayer:

Scripture: Mark 9:50 – Useful Love

Salt is excellent for seasoning. But if salt becomes tasteless, how can its flavor ever be restored? Your lives, like salt, are to season and preserve. So do not lose your flavor and preserve the peace in your union with one another. TPT

What do you hear from this scripture? What is God saying to you?

As I read and pray about this scripture, I hear several things. Although salt is one substance, it has several purposes. In this scripture, it states that salt is useful for seasoning and preserving. God created salt with purpose, just like us. We are born with God's purpose inside us.

The scripture also shows that it is possible for salt to lose its flavor and ultimately become useless. If, and when, salt loses its flavor, it is no longer useful to anything else. It cannot fulfill its purpose.

God is saying to me: be useful like salt. Whatever environment or situation I am in, season it and preserve it. Be useful for God's kingdom. As I am allowing God's Holy Spirit to use me, I am impacting the lives of others.

Reflection/Your Story:

This scripture is very relevant to me right now. I recently started a new job. After only being there about six weeks, I felt that it was time for me to leave. Although I had a job title,

I'd not been given any tasks or assignments. I felt useless and unproductive. I would pray and ask the Lord to use me in my work environment any way He could. I started noticing opportunities the Holy Spirit created for me to be "salt." I would have conversations with the employees and parents that required me to "Season and Preserve." Yielding myself to the Holy Spirit allowed me to share my faith and live in Christ. God began to show me how to be "salt" and share "useful love" to those I encountered. My last day at the job was on a Friday. God has another assignment for me. In my short time at the previous job, I met many new people and am hopeful these relationships will continue.

Activity:

1. Prayer – Spend time with the Lord talking and listening for wisdom, guidance, and instruction.
2. Practice – Being salt and sharing your flavor, God's love, wisdom, peace with others.
3. Praise – God for using you, allowing you to be salt, helping others.

Questions to Ponder:

1. Why am I here?
2. Who am I sent here for?
3. Am I still salty?
4. How can someone lose their salty flavor?

Prayer:

Heavenly Father, thank You for being salt in my life and allowing me to be salt in the lives of others. You created me in my mother's womb with and for a purpose, according to Jeremiah 1:5. I surrender my life to You so You can use me. Allow your love, peace, and wisdom to flow in and through me to others. May they feel Your presence when they encounter me, because you are in me. Holy Spirit, continue to teach me the ways of the Father. Lead me, guide me, and order my steps, so that my actions, words, and deeds are pleasing to the Lord. In Jesus' name!!! Amen.

Scripture: Gen 13:8 -Gracious Love

What do you hear from this scripture? What is God saying to you?

Reflection/Your Story:

Activity:

____

____

____

____

____

Questions to Ponder:

____

____

____

____

____

Prayer:

____

____

____

____

____

Scripture: Psalm 91:1-2 – Protective Love

He who dwells in the secret place of the Most High shall abide under the shadow of The Almighty. I will say of The LORD, "He is my refuge and my fortress; He is my God, in Him I will trust."

What do you hear from this scripture? What is God saying to you?

"The Most High"... Highest Above all. Accordingly, no person, place, or things (in this realm and all spiritual realms) are higher than Him. Nothing can reach us, and nothing can fall on us. This is our dwelling place of God Himself, The Most High. His Word describes our peaceful abode in Him, surrounded by His essence and glory, and forever embraced by Him in His love and home. THIS is the exemplary place of safety that nowhere on earth could ever match. This holy and marvelous *Person Place* has no equivalent and could not ever compare with our most treasured beloved ones (spouse, child, friend, or family). We live *There* now. We live *there* forever.

Reflection/Your Story:

Personally, I had to first fix my thoughts on His all-consuming sovereignty and safety as *The Most High* before I could fathom a real, secret dwelling place where God would actually receive someone like me. My horrible sins, neglects, compromises, pride, and foibles had created a target-magnet for unsettling and separating complications to fall on me (from the worldly and spiritual realms). Without any scolding, Lord Jesus drew me to His Word, revealing His accomplishments by His lood and His love for me. The more my relationship developed with Him, the more my faith grew until I realized this *Secret Place* was not something I would enter someday. Rather, I was in Him already. His work in me to will and to do His good pleasure, the Father's will (Philippians 2:13, Jeremiah 24:7) have been His constant. The effect of His work is causing confusion and every evil thing (James 3:16) to lose interest in my life and obscure their sight of me. His Spirit within me is guiding me to *follow* (and not struggle with Him). This is continuously strengthening my anchor to this beautiful truth: living safely, hidden in GOD, my refuge, my fortress... He is my invisible abode, my Beloved...how could I not trust Him? ...Yes, every moment as I grow, may my heart and mouth seamlessly repeat, "He is my GOD in whom I place all my trust."

Activity:

When alone with God, humble yourself and seek His heart for anything He wants to show you. Repentance is another form of worship where we give Him the sacrifice of our ways, wants, or what we used to think; and agree with His Love, which is His Will, Ways, and Wisdom. Don't be afraid. The Most High is safe. God is Love. His love covers all the sins of the world (1 John 2:2). Love died in your place. It's not about your behavior anymore. He's taken care of all that. He now makes everything be about you and Him being together...

forever. He is making you be like Him, and you will love the changes. Always be assured that He made you *on purpose*. Fling your whole being into Him in the Secret Place and stay.

Questions to ponder:

A suggestion to ask yourself: Sometimes, when I think people are ignoring me (as if they can't see me and are leaving me out), could it possibly be that God has hidden me from the view of the world and He is keeping me safe? (i.e., safe from trauma, accidents, gossip, temptations, and evil). Did it work?

Prayer:

Dear Father God, I ask in Lord Jesus' Name, that although I can't see You, touch You, or hear Your audible voice, please hold me closer to Your heart so I may really, really trust You. I believe You will do this, because You first desired this trust from me, and have been working to make it really happen. Thank You for waiting for me to come to this time in my life, when I would ask You for this deep, never-ending trust. Thank You for blessing me with Yourself. Thank You for loving me. I love You, too. Amen.

Scripture: Gen 13:8 -Gracious Love

What do you hear from this scripture? What is God saying to you?

Reflection/Your Story:

Activity:

Questions to Ponder:

Prayer:

Scripture: Matthew 5:9 – Peacemaker Love

Blessed are the peacemakers. For they shall be called the children of God.

What do you hear from this scripture? What is God saying to you?

Being a peacemaker for the Lord means that we as Christians engage in Godly activities to bring all of His people together despite their differences, misgivings, or shortcomings. We are promoting God's peace.

Reflection: Your Story:

As a registered nurse, I believe my career is my calling or ministry. As a younger nurse, I was more career-driven and thought of what I was doing as just a job. After maturing in Christ and going through some trials in my life, I was able to overcome these trials because of my relationship with Him. I began to pray for those that were about to have surgical procedures or just with people that requested me to. It took me a while to see that my profession was my ministry, because I encounter people every day in their most vulnerable state, and it doesn't matter if you are black or white, everyone wants to know that someone around them is a Christian. I found that I was so much happier to spread the Gospel of Jesus that now I will just pray with anyone who asks or if the spirit moves me to. I believe this is a way to bring those to Christ as a peacemaker. You don't have to give an elaborate prayer, but let others feel your sincerity when speaking to our Lord.

Activities:

Colossians: 1:20
John 3:16
John 16:33
Philippians 4:9
Corinthians 13:11

Questions to ponder:

1. During difficult times, ask yourself: What would Jesus do?
2. How can I be a peacemaker in my everyday life?
3. When people see me, do they see a peacemaker or a disruptor?
4. Who are those you consider peacemakers in your life, and what have you learned from them?
5. Remember, we are created in God's own image. You've got this!!!

Prayer:

Heavenly Father, please teach me how to become a peacemaker, whether it be in my own family, job, or community. May those that I encounter on a daily basis see You in me. May they see the struggles, the highs, and lows, but may they also see the VICTORY!! For all the days of my life, AMEN!!! Choose Jesus as your Christ and Savior today.

Scripture: Gen 13:8 -Gracious Love

____

____

____

____

____

What do you hear from this scripture? What is God saying to you?

____

____

____

____

____

Reflection/Your Story:

____

____

____

____

____

Activity:

Questions to Ponder:

Prayer:

Scripture: 1 Corinthians 1:3 – Truthful Love

Grace be unto you, and peace from God our Father, and from the Lord Jesus Christ.

What do you hear from this scripture? What is God saying to you?

God is reminding me that He is my all and all. He is the one I should go to and put my faith in. Because of God's grace, love, trust, and faith in Him, I will be blessed with His peace and love.

Reflection/Your Story:

At 75 years of age, I have been blessed in so many ways. But not always have I deserved God's blessings. Because of His love for me, I love my family wholeheartedly in a way that God will be pleased. I have also learned to be willing to sometimes put aside my desires for others. I am a work in progress. When I feel scared, worried, or upset, I know to pray and to put my faith in God and to always thank God for His grace and mercy.

No one is unwanted by God. His love for us is constant and never fails. As a child, I had polio, and without the faith my parents had in God, I might not be walking today. I was involved in the group that took the vaccine for polio victims. My parents taught me early to pray and have faith and it is God's will for all of our prayers to be answered. I have always tried to remember this and instill this in my family, whether biologically or those God has blessed me to have in my life.

Activity:

Let others know how God's grace has kept me and not just keep it to myself.

Embrace my walk with God.

Make more time for Bible study.

Questions to Ponder:

What makes a person beautiful in God's eyes?

How does prayer bring me closer to God?

Prayer:

God our Father, thank You for all of my blessings. They have been numerous. This nation is in so much turmoil, and I am asking that You heal the land. God, bless my family and please keep Your hands of protection upon them.

Please keep us safe from all hurt, harm, and danger. We know that You are in control, even if we sometimes feel You are far away. Thank You for health and strength, for friends, and for freedom to worship. Bless us all and keep us all. I ask in Your sons' name, Amen.

Scripture: Gen 13:8 -Gracious Love

What do you hear from this scripture? What is God saying to you?

Reflection/Your Story:

Activity:

Questions to Ponder:

Prayer:

Scripture: Numbers 12:8 – Humble Love

With him will I speak mouth to mouth, even apparently, and not in dark speeches; and the similitude of the Lord shall he behold: wherefore.

What do you hear from this scripture? What is God saying to you?

What I hear from this scripture is that we often criticize or talk down on people when they mess up or when we don't understand them. But God sees us for who we are, everyone should be treated the way God treats us. Once you have a relationship with God, the way you talk will change. God wants you as a friend, He wants you to hear His voice and bring clarity to your life. You should only listen to the voice of God.

Reflection/Your Story:

Reflecting on this scripture, there have been times that I may have spoken ungodly words about someone or criticized them when I should not have.

I have been humble with my kids. I had to learn to listen to them and admit my shortcomings and mistakes. I have learned that just because I am the parent, I still need to show vulnerability. It has made our relationship so strong and allows for open communication and trust between us.

Activity:

With every person you encounter, think about how God talks to you and how God treats you. Develop a closer relationship with God so that all you hear is His voice, so people may see Him through you.

Questions to Ponder:

How is your relationship with God?
Do you hear His voice clearly?
What steps do you think you should take to get there?

Prayer:

Father God, change our life, help us to become closer and to become Your friend. I pray that we don't criticize others; man looks at the outer appearance, but God looks at the heart. Let us be quick to hear and slow to speak. In Jesus' name, Amen.

Scripture: Gen 13:8 -Gracious Love

What do you hear from this scripture? What is God saying to you?

Reflection/Your Story:

Activity:

Questions to Ponder:

Prayer:

Scripture: Psalm 56:5 – Dependable Love

Day after day cruel critics distort my words; constantly they plot my collapse. TPT

All day long they twist my words and say hurtful things. AMP

All day long they twist my words; all their schemes are for my ruin. NIV

Every day they wrest my words: All their thoughts are against me for evil. KJV

What do you hear from this scripture? What is God saying to you?

All day, any day, every day, every opportunity others will see me/you based on their limitations and speak from that place. This is corrupt and twisted. They don't care about what's coming from your mouth, but think their words/opinions matter more. Words either are life or death, blessing or curses. The tongue is corrupt, unless you know Jesus and speak what He says.

Reflection/Your Story:

I can share several stories from my life. Now I'm in a work environment where I have an immediate supervisor, then they have a supervisor. Well, I've only been there less than a year and in some areas, I still ask a question to do my job in excellence. Well, the big boss is a dictator and oppressor. She speaks to you like you are ignorant. So I pause, walk away, go pray and talk to the Lord and present my case to Him. It's not right, and in Genesis when He said to dominate, that's not what He meant. So I do my job excellently, but always keep communication with God, my Father, open. I express my corrections to her in respect.

In another situation, I was in ministry for fifteen years; I was never noticed unless it sounded like Pastor's words. Even though I would speak what the Lord said, it was twisted or perverted. I've had an amazing relationship with the Lord since I was small or young in age. I went through a horrible situation that brought my voice forward and bold. Now I am heard because God puts me on the frontline and sets me where He wants me.

Activity:

1. You practice speaking kindness to yourself.
2. You practice speaking kindness over/to others.
3. Find out what words God speaks toward you.

Questions to Ponder:

Why do others say one thing, but do something totally different?

What do people feel they govern/lord/tower over others? They're not Jehovah!

Why is it easier to speak negatively than positively?

Prayer:

Father of my peace and composure, I come to you in Jesus' name. I thank You, Father, for who You have created me to be. I thank You for loving me continually and unconditionally. Your love for/to me is dependable. I depend on it, consistently trust it, and won't live without it. I depend on Your breath for living. I depend on Your ways for guidance. I depend on Your love to comfort me. Thank You for who You are. Your word will not return to You void. You spoke me into existence. Keep your hand on/around/before me. I love you, in Jesus' name…Amen (Hallelujah).

Scripture: Gen 13:8 -Gracious Love

____

____

____

____

____

What do you hear from this scripture? What is God saying to you?

____

____

____

____

____

Reflection/Your Story:

____

____

____

____

____

Activity:

Questions to Ponder:

Prayer:

Scripture: Proverbs 27:17 – Tough Love

It takes a grinding wheel to sharpen a blade, and so one person sharpens the character of another. TPT

What do you hear from this scripture? What is God saying to you?

In most churches and Bible studies I have attended, I have learned a lot about God and what I could do for God. I was raised in a rules-based church and lost my faith in God. I realized later that I lost my faith in the church because the rules were different in different countries. When I heard Graham Kerr, a British, gourmet chef say that he needed Jesus, my thought was, "If that sophisticated man needs Jesus, so do I." So I told God that I would read the Bible and do what He wanted. Needless to say, the Bible became a rulebook for me and everyone else. And, of course, I started in the Old Testament. I liked the part of the Psalms where David cursed his enemies, but not the parts where he lauded God. I did not realize that it was no longer a church of, "An eye for an eye, a tooth for a tooth." It was all about forgiveness and turning the other cheek. Turning the other cheek in Aramaic means to not fight about an afront.

Reflection/Your Story:

I used to think I was so wise when I would ask God to send people's curses back on them. In my relationship of love with God, I have learned to really bless those who hurt me and others instead of asking for their curses to be visited upon them. Now my favorite prayer is: Lord, let all curses fall flat and bless both the sender and the receiver a thousand-fold instead.

It took me a long time to realize that Jesus died not only for our forgiveness, but also for a relationship with a triune God – Father, Jesus, and Holy Spirit. Jesus died so the Father would see us as He sees Jesus, without sin. And it's only the Holy Spirit in me that can give me the grace to see others with the Father's eyes. It's awesome to see others as God sees them in spite of the way they may be acting out. I do believe that I need the Holy Spirit to open my eyes to see beyond another person's actions; but one of the most important things I have learned is to love myself. God is an awesome God and He created me in His image, so I guess that makes me awesome. When I know who I am in God, I don't need to try to please others to get them to love me.

I'm still far from perfect as I continue to find out that I hurt others when I get triggered by something they have said, done, or didn't do. I've learned that there are parts of me that were wounded as children and are still being prompted by the enemy to protect themselves in ungodly ways. I've learned to find myself as a little one who was hurt as a child and not comforted. I hold that part of me, if she allows, and comfort her. I ask her if it would be okay for the Lord to unburden her of her pain from her trauma.

It's awesome to see a wounded part of myself free to be the child she was created to be. The fruit of bringing hurt parts of me to the Lord is freedom from being reactive.

Prayer:

Lord, I ask that You would lead all of us to the knowledge that You did create us in Your image, and that You love each one of us as a unique individual, and we need not judge ourselves according to what others are doing. We all have our own unique gifts. Help us to become aware of them and with the Holy Spirit, let those gifts bless others. Thank you for loving us, and let that love flow out to others.

Scripture: Gen 13:8 -Gracious Love

What do you hear from this scripture? What is God saying to you?

Reflection/Your Story:

Activity:

Questions to Ponder:

Prayer:

Scripture: Malachi 2:7 – Knowing Love

"For the lips of priests ought to preserve knowledge, because he is the messenger of the Lord Almighty and people seek instruction from his mouth."

What do you hear from this scripture? What is God saying to you?

The scripture says that priests, who are messengers of God, should teach and guard His truth because they were the keepers of truth and guides for people. In context with the scriptures that come before and after verse seven, the Lord reminds the priests of His covenant with Levi, who walked with Him in peace, reverence, and uprightness. He warns and exposes the priests who have begun to tolerate and participate in the unlawful behavior of the people of Israel. Because the priests had become corrupt, they caused many people to stumble.

God is reminding and warning me to "watch yourself, girl!" Be mindful to not be corrupted or distracted by everything our culture deems as right and acceptable. Examine His truth, and live by it. Love corrects.

Reflection/Your Story:

I'm still hopeful and encouraged because God's promise of a future king who would come to redeem, purify, and offer salvation to the world continues to be true today as it was for the people of Israel during the time of the prophet Malachi. Just like the priests are God's representative to the people, I am Christ's representative to my family, and if I become corrupted, it's likely that my children may follow. Just as He warned and disciplined the people of Israel when they sinned against Him, He demonstrated His love for them by not leaving them in their sin. In the same manner today, Christ does the same for me and my children. As a mother, I have chosen to love my children with full knowledge that they are going to misbehave and make mistakes. "But even if we are faithless, he will still be full of faith, for he never wavers in his faithfulness to us!" (2 Timothy 2:3).

My story is quite simple. I lived a life that was mostly a lie. I ascribed to what culture and society said that I was or should be until I was introduced to Jesus in a way that was relatable, real, and practical, and I began establishing my own personal relationship with Him.

I was introduced to Christ as a young adult woman and learned about His life, death, burial, and resurrection in a way that was not condemning, but redemptive. It displayed His humanity and revealed about the lengths to which He went to save me, and that He loved me. I chose to believe that He is the Son of God sent to save us. And when I heard about what forgiveness of sin could do for my life because Christ did it for me first, it pricked my conscience, released, and then freed me from unforgiveness, bitterness, self-recrimination, and self-destructive behavior so that I could then extend forgiveness to the man who hurt me as a child. Because I was learning about Him and the practical applications of the scriptures to my everyday life, I was transformed. My heart had by this time softened, and my head and heart were aligned with Christ's, so I said yes to the invitation for Him to change my life (repent, seek forgiveness, and acknowledge Him as Lord and Savior). I chose to live for Him because He first loved me!

Activity:

Scripture of the Day, Week, or Month

Purpose: To know and learn Christ's instruction on love to be able to see it growing in some measure, as a reflection of God's character in your life because of daily practice.

In a special notebook or journal, write the following scripture that Paul instructs us about **love** — for God, each other, and ourselves:

"Love is patient, love is kind. It does not envy, it does not boast, it is not proud. It does not dishonor others, it is not self-seeking, it is not easily angered, and it keeps no record of wrongs. Love does not delight in evil but rejoices with the truth. It always protects, always trusts, always hopes, and always perseveres. Love never fails" (1 Corinthians 13:4-8a).

Memorize that scripture and meditate on it for the length of time that you specify.

Draw or sketch or doodle what comes to mind as you meditate on the scripture if it helps with memorization. One does not need to be an artist for this activity. Another approach to memorizing the scripture(s) is to put it in a song. I was amazed at the scriptures I memorized while playing Bible songs for children to my young children. Also, for context, try to read the preceding and proceeding scripture(s).

Questions to Ponder:

1. How can I apply Paul's instructions on love in my life in practical ways?
2. What are some examples in the bible of God demonstrating His love for us by correcting us?

Prayer:

Dear Heavenly Father, hallowed be thy name. Thank You for this day that You had made and for granting me another day of life. I am grateful for Your goodness, faithfulness, and love towards us at all times and for transforming our lives. As You've done for others, I pray and ask that You continue to extend your grace, patience, and loving kindness to me. Help me to do the same for my fellow man. Please forgive me of my sins. Giving You all the glory and honor. In Jesus' name, Amen!

Scripture: Gen 13:8 -Gracious Love

____

____

____

____

____

What do you hear from this scripture? What is God saying to you?

____

____

____

____

____

Reflection/Your Story:

____

____

____

____

____

Activity:

Questions to Ponder:

Prayer:

Scripture: Proverbs 13:3 – Wise Love

He that keepeth his mouth keepeth his life; but he that openeth wide his lips shall have destruction. Guard your words and you'll guard your life, but if you don't control your tongue it will ruin everything.

What do you hear from this scripture? What is God saying to you?

One's words can fill one's life with good fruit or ruin your life, so I should watch what I say because my life depends on what I release from my mouth. And I feel God is saying that my words set the path and direction of my life, be it positive or negative.

Reflection/Your Story:

James 3:6 says that the tongue is a fire, a world of iniquity. It defiles the whole body and sets on fire the course of nature.

James 3:8 says the tongue can no man tame; it is an unruly evil, yet verse ten says out of the same mouth proceeds blessing and cursing.

In my life, I have released words that weren't right; they may have even been misleading due to the lack of knowledge in God's word. His word says in 1 Corinthians 13:11, "When I was a child, I spoke as a child and understood as a child." But when I came to know the Lord and His words in a more intimate way, I put away childish things. My words became words of love and wisdom (no longer me, but He) who speaks through me. So now when I speak, I choose my words wisely so they edify, not break down.

Song: Tis so sweet to trust in Jesus
Just to take Him at His word
Just to rest upon His promise
Just to know: Thus saith The Lord!

I'm so glad I learned to trust Him. I know He's with me now and forevermore (Psalm 19:14).

Activity:

1. Take a day a week to release only positive and encouraging words.
2. Love no matter what for an entire day unconditionally.
3. Pray for someone other than yourself.

Questions to Ponder:

What would happen if I spoke encouraging words all day?

What does Wise love look like in my day-to-day life?

What is Wise love? Do we all possess it, if not how can we obtain it?

Prayer:

Heavenly Father, teach me to say and pray Your words. Give me wisdom and understanding to be more like Thee. Let my words be full of love and kindness. Let them forever lead to You. In Jesus' name I pray, Amen.

Scripture: Gen 13:8 -Gracious Love

What do you hear from this scripture? What is God saying to you?

Reflection/Your Story:

Activity:

____

____

____

____

____

Questions to Ponder:

____

____

____

____

____

Prayer:

____

____

____

____

____

Scripture: Psalm 34:13 – Uncorrupt Love

KJV Keep thy tongue from evil, and thy lips from speaking guile.

TPT Do you want to live a long, good life, enjoying beauty that fills each day? Then never speak a lie or allow wicked words to come from your mouth.

WHAT DO YOU HEAR FROM THIS SCRIPTURE? WHAT IS IT SAYING TO YOU?

As we have only one tongue. God had a plan in doing so, it's a gateway. Words are produced by our tongue. They flow out—good and/or evil.

These words can be informative, foolish, hurtful, corrective, the truth, or a lie.

In the KJV, the writing is straightforward and emphatic. It's a command by God, rather than a coercion, suggestion, or request. This makes it known to the reader that God is not allowing wiggle room.

The TPT indicates an attempt to get one's attention with a somewhat rhetorical question. Who wouldn't want these pleasantries that were significant in one's future or outcome in life? This scripture doesn't mix words in the solution. It refers to opening the door to release these malicious, sinful and downright unrighteous words would negate part of the verse.

Luke 6:46: "And why call me Lord Lord and do not what I say."

Matthew 12:34 says, "Out of the abundance of the heart of the heart the mouth speaks."

Psalm 104:4 says, "A forward (contrary) heart shall depart from me; I will not know a wicked person."

Sin separates us from God whether in mind, word, or deed. This means our words will line up with what we say because it is a heart matter.

James 3:11 says, "Does a fountain send forth at the same place, sweet water and bitter."

James 17:17 says, "Sanctify them by the truth; your word is truth. So those with the heart of God reframe from lies and falsehoods as we know holiness without no man shall see God."

Since God's word is truth and we're set apart by the washing by the water of the word, we as believers will not trip up and lie as the liar is not in us.

REFLECTION

Raised in a home and family that was "church-minded," I spent all of my formative years in the house of God. I was baptized in the Baptist church at 10 years old. I was immensely involved in the Sunday school and was the BYTU rep for my church. I loved singing in the junior, then as I grew up, senior choir. However, I wasn't saved. No one even talked about a salvation call or surrendering your life to Jesus, according to Romans 10:9-10. But because my mother had passed when I was ten, I had a lot of love and guidance there in the church.

Being my father worked all the time and was a good provider, my siblings and I were left to our own monitoring. I was molested four times as a child, and this changed my heart.

But I still was churchy and very outgoing in school with sports and other activities. However, it caused hurt, mistrust, and I doubted my identity. I became a people pleaser and covert manipulator to avoid harm, as I couldn't tell my father as he would have used lethal recompense to resolve the matter. I lived a lie. It was my protective mechanism, because of the secrets. Yes, lies will and secrets can go hand in hand, saying, "I'll take it to my grave." However, that's the enemy's territory and guilt, shame, and nonsocial, ungodly beliefs, bitterroot judgments, anger, and lack of trust were my portion.

ACTIVITY TO ENCOURAGE OR HELP WORK IT OUT

Lies can come in various facets.

It can be mixed or half-truth. Others are embellishing the truth, twisting the truth, hiding the truth within, living a lie and a flat-out lie, and some not mentioned here. These strongholds and their influence and activity in one's life must be dispelled by a relationship with Jesus Christ as Lord and Savior, eating the word like a delicacy and a fervent prayer life. Love is the greatest gift. First Corinthians 13:4-7 is where I would go next to let them know what Godly love is not worldly, fake, or self-hate. To find out that there is a loving God that does not condemn us or forsake us. Inviting them to lunch and other non-church activities, embracing their children, being patient, sharing personal occurrences (being transparent), and correcting wrong and stinking thinking. Making it clear that lying to get social services, income tax, someone else's spouse, and so much more without judging or putting down is of the devil who the Bible says is a liar and the father of lies.

In John 14:6, it says, "I am the way, the truth, and the life." Is The Truth living, residing, and moving in our life? No man comes to the Father but by Him. No one can come to the Father but through Jesus Christ, and He stands at the door of our heart knocking. What will be the outcome? Do we want all the pigs out of our parlor and be one of those referred to as being a child of God, free and whole? This life is but a vapor. We want to live and reign eternally with the lover of our soul, and His father our maker.

" These are they who have come out of the great tribulation; and have washed their robes and made them white in the Blood of the Lamb" (Revelation 7:14 NKJV).

Anything that is not like God will be revealed with the word and fervent prayer if we are His. We can be washed whiter than snow by our relationship with Jesus and doing whatever in our power to be a vessel of honor. Not one that's aligned with the wiles of the enemy.

PRAYER

Father, in the name of Jesus, we thank You for who You are in our lives. Master, Savior, Lord. Your Word says the steps of a good man are ordered of the Lord. Give us a heart of surrender that we will stay the course and plan that You have preordained for us. For, Father, we know that death and life is in the power of the tongue, and we will eat the fruit thereof. So, Father, let the words of our mouth and the meditations of our heart be acceptable in your sight, oh Lord, my strength and my redeemer. We bind lying and the lying spirit that would cause You to turn away from our sin. Moreover, Father, we don't want to miss the glorious life You have promised Your children if we are obedient in all our ways. We know the enemy comes to steal, kill, and destroy. He is a liar and the father of lies, so right now, in the name of Jesus, we renounce, bind, and cast out all spirits tied to the lying spirit. We speak healing to those areas that life has invaded in us, whether by our sin of lying or by the trauma that caused us to feel the need to lie or align with Satan and his imps and we set the ax to the taproot and command it to upchuck, wither, and die. I command you, Satan, to walk in dry places as you have no authority over the lives of those that are in Christ Jesus. Father, we know the heart is desperately wicked above all things and who could know it. Father, we will ingest Psalm 51 that You would cast us not away from Your presence nor take Your Holy Spirit away from us. Purge us, Lord, and wash us whiter than snow. Give us a mind to walk out our deliverance and healing and let us work out our own soul salvation with fear and trembling, that we would be living epistles, read of all men. In Jesus' name we pray. Amen.

Scripture: Gen 13:8 -Gracious Love

What do you hear from this scripture? What is God saying to you?

Reflection/Your Story:

Activity:

____

____

____

____

____

Questions to Ponder:

____

____

____

____

____

Prayer:

____

____

____

____

____

Scripture: James 3:2 – Growing Love

We all in many areas, but especially with our words. Yet if we're able to bridle (control) ourselves in every way, and that means our character is mature and fully developed.

What do you hear from this scripture? What is God saying to you?

This scripture is a parallel reference to Prov. 18:21. Over many years, my words have been silenced. Not knowing that I had potential powers to help save or persuade someone to life. God is working with me on this. Earlier I expressed that I did not care anymore. Let me clarify exactly what that means. I now have a holy boldness to say what God tells me to say to people. I thought that those that walked longer with Christ had the right to control me. Although the Lord has been speaking to me for years, I will no longer silence the words given to me.

Reflection/Your Story:

My story is a TV show series. I would call these shows "The Act of Bravery." I am in such a timein my life right now. There is nowhere I can move without the Spirit of the Lord. I have my struggles and overcame some of them. The story is still being told.

A time when God was growing in my life is when I had made the decision that I wanted to move out of my mother's home at twenty-six. I had become comfortable with how I was living. The day I realized that I was going to my own place was to trust and believe that God was going to provide that for me. I began to press in and truly ask for specific things to be broken off my life. God's hand began to move first inside where there were things keeping me in bondage. He began teaching me about budgeting and saying no to those things that were keeping me in the same place. The love and grace God extended to me allowed for chains to be broken off. Knowing that my family will be okay if I'm not there helped. I was expected to take control of my life. God had bigger and better things for me to do besides babysitting my family. When I finally moved out, I dedicated my place to His spirit and gave full control. For those whom enter that they feel the love of the Father and peace of His spirit.

Activity:

Start with the person closest to you.

Questions to Ponder:

What are you willing to sacrifice to receive?

Prayer:

Lord, exchange my mind for yours. Help my words to become your words. Jesus, silence the fear in my heart. Allow me to embrace those things that I am afraid of and do it anyway while scared. Lord, let Your bravery be mine. Let your heart sow in me so that my words come only from You. In Jesus' name!!

Scripture: Gen 13:8 -Gracious Love

____

____

____

____

____

What do you hear from this scripture? What is God saying to you?

____

____

____

____

____

Reflection/Your Story:

____

____

____

____

____

Activity:

Questions to Ponder:

Prayer:

Scripture: Proverb 18:21 – Consequential Love

Death and Life are in the power of the tongue and they that love it shall eat the fruit thereof.

What do you hear from this scripture? What is God saying to you?

The tongue is a sword. It speaks life and death. People say things about you and your family. You cannot hurt me without hurting yourself in the word. I live for me, not people. I am a strong woman of God.

Reflection/Your Story:

People talk about each other all the time. There are words that have been said about me and my family, but it never hurt us.

Activity:

Be strong in the Lord. Keep God first and pray for those who can't pray for themselves. It's a whole lot of people to encourage and need to know Jesus.

Questions to Ponder:

Why do people say things about each other instead of praying for each other? (We are all God's children.)

Prayer:

Hear my voice, O God. In my prayer, preserve my life from fear of the enemy. Hide me from the secret counsel of the wicked. Heavenly Father, forgive those that speak ill of people, their life, and their situations. Forgive us all where we failed. We are to be on the mark. Keep us in Your word and encourage us. In Jesus' name… Amen.

Scripture: Gen 13:8 -Gracious Love

What do you hear from this scripture? What is God saying to you?

Reflection/Your Story:

Activity:

Questions to Ponder:

Prayer:

Scripture: Psalm 51:12 – Abiding Love

Iron sharpens iron, so a man sharpens the countenance of his friend.

What do you hear from this scripture? What is God saying to you?

When I think about iron, I think first about how iron is made, how it is crafted. What is it crafted to do? Immediately, I think of fire. Fire purifies, hardens, and cleanses out all impurities. As iron is being made or crafted, I know it goes through intense heat and fire to harden the steel/iron. It can only be sharpened and hardened by being put in the fire. If the heat is not hot enough, the steel/iron breaks and is not able to be used for what it is intended. As it is in the natural, so it is in the spiritual. I know that God has created, crafted me with a purpose and destiny to fulfill. In order to do that, I MUST go through the fire. I must be tested and proven. Because His love abides in me, and I'm abiding in Him, I can have peace and confidence, knowing He loves me and is fulfilling His plans in and through me. Only once I've been refined in the fire am I able to "sharpen" my friends and those I encounter in this life, giving them hope and assurance that God's abiding love will carry and sustain them even in the midst of the fire.

Reflection/Your Story

When I was 35, my father passed away on February 25. My husband passed away on August 11, my birthday. Two of the most important men in my life were gone. I was angry with God; I didn't understand how He "let" it happen. I had faith, I believed in healing, and I almost always believed and knew God loved me. So how could "HE" have let this happen? I was left with three small children with no income, no life insurance, and no job. All of the couple friends in the church didn't feel "comfortable" now with just me. I was left alone, no financial help, no emotional help, just myself and God, who I was angry with. I couldn't worship, I couldn't praise, I was afraid. In my complaining one morning, I said to mysel, "If my father was still alive, he'd help take care of me." Immediately, I heard the Holy Spirit speak to me, "I am your Father and I will take care of you. Do you trust me?" You see, I had rested in His abiding love my entire life. My earthly father was a perfect example of how my Heavenly Father loved me, cared for me, provided for me, so it had always been very easy **for me to trust God. Yet here I was, putting my trust more** in my earthly father than I was in my Heavenly Father. From that moment, something changed in me. I began to open my heart again to giving and receiving. I began to worship again. God never failed me. He provided for me physically and spiritually in every way it was needed. I experienced complete isolation from those I had called friends. I had needed the "iron" of them to give me hope, give me love, and encouragement. BUT GOD!! It is only because of His abiding love that I came through the fire.

Activity:

1. Study the Word, live in the Word. It will be life to you when no one else is around.
2. Surround yourself with friends who don't just say "YES" to everything you want to do or say. Have friends who are courageous enough to say NO when it needs to be said. This is how we are sharpened.

Questions to ponder:

1. When I'm in the fire, who or what do I reflect?
2. When I come out, will I smell like smoke?
3. Do I get angry with God when I'm in the fire?
4. Who do I turn to when I'm in the middle of the fire?

Prayer

Father, thank You for loving me and abiding in me. Your love carries me and sustains me even in the midst of the fire. Thank You that You have a plan and purpose for me that can only be fulfilled as I am tested and proven. I trust You to bring me through. Thank You for surrounding me with Godly men and women to speak truth into my life. You are a good, good Father and I give You praise!

Scripture: Gen 13:8 -Gracious Love

____

____

____

____

____

What do you hear from this scripture? What is God saying to you?

____

____

____

____

____

Reflection/Your Story:

____

____

____

____

____

Activity:

Questions to Ponder:

Prayer:

Scripture: Romans 12:2 – Transforming Love

And be not conformed to this world: but be ye transformed by the renewing of your mind, that ye may prove what is that good, and acceptable, and perfect, will of God.

Reflection/Your Story:

Renewing my mind daily to discern what is good; do not conform to this world because this world is evil.

Activity:

Think on good things, things that are pure, and take on the mind of Christ. Let this mind be in you that is also in Christ Jesus. He will keep you in perfect peace if you keep your mind stayed on him.

Questions to Ponder:

So many scriptures come to mind when it talks about your mind. The battle begins in your mind. The helmet of salvation protects our minds. As a man thinks so is he. Renew your thinking and take on the mind of Christ.

Prayer:

My prayer is that my mind will be renewed and that I will take on the mind of Christ.

Let this mind be in you that is also in Christ Jesus. He will keep you in perfect peace if you keep your mind stayed on him. Amen.

Scripture: Gen 13:8 -Gracious Love

What do you hear from this scripture? What is God saying to you?

Reflection/Your Story:

Activity:

Questions to Ponder:

Prayer:

Scripture: 2 Corinthians 4:16 – Renewed Love

NIV – Therefore we do not lose heart. Though outwardly we are wasting away, yet inwardly we are being renewed day by day.

AMP – Therefore we do not become discouraged (spiritless, disappointed, or afraid). Though our self is (progressively) wasting away, yet our inner self is being (progressively) renewed day by day.

KJV – For which cause we faint not, but though our outward man perish(die), yet the inward man is renewed day by day.

TPT – So no wonder we don't give up. For even though our outer person gradually wears out, our inner being is renewed every single day. We view our slight, short-lived troubles in the light of eternity. We see our difficulties as the substance that produces for us an eternal, weighty glory far beyond all comparison because we don't focus our attention on what is seen but on what is unseen. For what is seen is temporary, but the unseen realm is eternal.

What do you hear from this scripture? What is God saying to you?

Don't give up/throw in the towel, nor cancel God's blessings. Our outer man goes from baby to elderly. A natural, pure state to tattered/abuse/misuse/misunderstood/heartache back to a pure state. Although in the natural, the world makes getting older look bad, it's a gift to go from glory to glory, grace to grace. All the while we become closer and closer to our maker, God.

Reflection/Your Story:

I was in a season where I was in need. I started in a healthy relationship with the Lord and was totally in love with Him. I guess my fellow believers at the church where I belong felt that it was time to marry. They proposed a guy that initially I despised because of his character. We were court-approved by our pastors and went through counseling. The entire journey there was "red" flags. But I was so invested that I believed we could grow into what God desired of us. We were eventually married. I was so numb to it all; I do not even remember the day. He wanted a trophy and "The Green Card." Meaning accolades or things are seen that have no value. I tried to be supportive and encouraging. I even invested all I had into the start-up of his business. He took and took and took, then damaged everything else. The destructive, sabotage spirit was prevalent. After we said, "I Do," he flipped a 180 back to himself. He came very verbally abusive, belittling, and destructive. I never knew what face/person I would awaken to. After six months, I stopped working with him and got two jobs. I knew it was coming to an end. I felt like I was in a never-ending hole that sucked all life out of me. I went to the ER twice, and I am a very healthy person who has never gone to the ER. I left after ten months of asking God for a way out. He moved quickly on my behalf. Our covenant ended after one year. Little did I know, he was a narcissist! No one really knew him in our church, even though they said they did. He had no accountability, no friends, and no family to account for him. Anything I would try to build, he would try to sabotage. I am so grateful that my Jesus was with me through it all. It could have been worse. I went through counseling to release and had some heart-to-heart times with the Lord. The Lord raised me up to be able to help other women in the same situation get free. The Lord has renewed my love for him and my inner circle, but most of all me. I longed for Jesus so much and now am back in place/relationship with my Jesus.

Activity:

- After eating the mango, keep the seed and give two days.
- Cut the seed open (God wants to bring out what He put in us to grow and prosper).
- Wrap the seed in a moist towel and place in a ziplock (He wants to shield us).
- After three weeks, it starts to sprout (It's a process, not quick).
- After five weeks, plant into potting soil to grow (The outcome is more beautiful, powerful, and renewed in Christ).

Questions to Ponder:

1. Does God give up hope on us?
2. Is God always with us?
3. How is love renewed?
4. When mistakes are made, what now?

Renewed: *Revive, come back to, restore, reaffirm*

Love: *fondness, attachment, care, concern, kindness, romance*

Prayer:

Holy Father, in Jesus' name, thank You for who You are. Thank You for creating me in Your image, after Your likeness. Where I missed it, You always caught me. You have had and still have a plan and purpose for me. May I walk out Your ways, being a light and sharing my faith. You knew where I would falter, and You always welcomed me back with open arms. Your love is renewing and continuous. I pray Your renewed love is felt through my words. All glory, honor, and praise are Yours. In Jesus' name… Amen!

Scripture:

*John 3:5-7 *2 Corinthians 5:17

Scripture: Gen 13:8 -Gracious Love

____

____

____

____

____

What do you hear from this scripture? What is God saying to you?

____

____

____

____

____

Reflection/Your Story:

____

____

____

____

____

Activity:

Questions to Ponder:

Prayer:

Scripture: Ephesians 4:23 – Active Love

And be continually renewed in the spirit of your mind [having a fresh, untarnished mental and spiritual attitude].

Ephesians 4:23 AMP

To take a fresh breath and to let God renew your attitude and spirit.

Ephesians 4:23 VOICE

Instead, let the Spirit renew your thoughts and attitudes.

Ephesians 4:23 NL

And you must let your spirits and minds keep being renewed.

Ephesians 4:23 CJB

Let the Spirit change your way of thinking.

Ephesians 4:23 CEV

What do you hear from this scripture? What is God saying to you?

This is a stark reminder to not trust my thoughts unless they've been filtered by the Word of God. He is my Father and loves me right into my destiny!

Reflection/Your Story:

Because I'm a deep thinker and tend to analyze pretty much most things I encounter or deal with…it's easy to just want to go with the findings of my analysis thinking I'm making a loving decision for myself and proceed from there. I've learned over the years through my walk with God that moving in this fashion is quite dangerous! It's like trying to navigate a minefield at night without night-vision goggles and a minesweeper. After experiencing several unnecessary self-inflicted (because I trusted my thoughts) catastrophes…I started simply sifting "my" analyses through God's Word and only what was originated by Him made the cut! As I realized and totally acknowledged that God IS LOVE and through his Word He would actively guide me starting with shaping my thought life...things started to flow so much better in every area of my life than they ever had before!

Activity:

Start each day with scripture…at least one and use it as a set point for the day. Look it up in several different translations. Memorize it…allow it to challenge your thoughts by reminding yourself that God is His Word and He is Love. As you do this daily… you're building an arsenal that will serve you well! Think of it as sifting flour for a nice, scrumptious pound cake! You're getting out all of the lumps to ensure that your finished product will be pleasing to all you serve it to.

Questions to Ponder:

Are my thoughts being filtered by the Word of God? Do I really trust that My Creator knows and loves me better than I know and love myself?

Prayer:

I thank You, Lord, that because I choose to filter my thoughts through Your Word…my mind is being changed and renewed daily! Your Spirit is leading my spirit…my thoughts are lining up with Your thoughts…I have the mind of Christ! I Am Loved and I Am Grateful!

Scripture: Gen 13:8 -Gracious Love

What do you hear from this scripture? What is God saying to you?

Reflection/Your Story:

Activity:

____

____

____

____

____

Questions to Ponder:

____

____

____

____

____

Prayer:

____

____

____

____

____

Scripture: Psalm 145:20 – Preserving Love

The Lord watches over all who love Him, but all the wicked, He will destroy. NIV

What do you hear from this scripture? What is God saying to you?

Lord, atch all who love you. (But God will destroy the wicked and sinful.) What God is saying to me is that He is watching me. His eyes are on me because I love Him, but the wicked will be destroyed. That leaves me out if I continue to love Him.

Reflection/Your Story:

I have seen the Lord watch over me all my life; from my existence until this present moment. How Satan wanted my life from birth, difficult situations, doubt, and fear. My love for Him was secure and His watch was constant even when I didn't think He saw or was there, but He was and still is.

I remember my dad was very ill in the hospital and the time of his departure was any day. I got out of my bed so as not to disturb my husband and went to another bedroom. I prayed to my God and cried bitterly. The lights were off, but I was aware that I wasn't alone. I sensed the presence of angels filling the room and God embracing me while I lay in His arms. Hallelujah!!!

Activity:

Read scripture daily. Reflect on His goodness and journal.

Questions to Ponder:

How was God watching me?
Who and what did God use to show His love to me?
How did I react to His Love?
What can I do to show Him love?

The definition for persevering is steadfast; to persist in a state, enterprise, or undertaking in spite of counter influences, opposition, or discouragement.

Examples of His persevering love: The sun is shining every day, clouds and a beautiful blue sky. Every night, the stars and moon are our light. He meets our daily needs. He is the same yesterday, today, and forever. He forgives us daily, over and over. His angels assist us daily. We lay down and He raises us up. Daily He thinks of us. Daily He works behind the scenes. Daily He has plans for us. He daily dances over us. He daily draws us near. He daily gives us peace. He daily hears our prayers. Daily He performs His promises. The wicked do not have His persevering love. He will destroy them, but He does not want to. Holy Spirit touches their hearts to love Him and He is more than willing to watch over them, too.

Prayer:

Father, thank You for Your watchful eye. You see me and You are everywhere at the same time. Your love for me will never change and Your watch will not stop. Holy Spirit, remind me of the Father's watchful eye that moves throughout the earth, seeing if there are those who are faithful. May I be the one. In Jesus' name!

Scripture: Gen 13:8 -Gracious Love

What do you hear from this scripture? What is God saying to you?

Reflection/Your Story:

Activity:

Questions to Ponder:

Prayer:

Scripture: Matthew 5:44 – International Love

"But I tell you, love your enemies and pray for those who persecute you…"

What do you hear from this scripture? What is God saying to you?

Extend love and empathy to those who are just as human as you. We all bear burdens; come from the same Creator. To harm and wish ill on others is to harm and wish ill on yourself/the Creator themselves.

Reflection/Your Story:

As I tirelessly fight for the freedom of others, I must also understand that it is divine intervention. It is beyond me. Beyond the physical. Freedom is not convenient or conventional. It demands the hearts of those who hurt. Maybe I and my enemies are fundamentally not so different. We all long to be seen. The Father handles us with the utmost compassion and gentleness; should we extend that same love to others? I would say yes to this over and over, but it is really difficult for me to walk that out when I feel there is moral injustice.

Activity:

Practice mindfulness and prayer. Be intentional instead of impulsively reactionary. State your boundaries. Encourage healthy conversations. It's less about influencing "said enemies," but more about understanding one another. It's not our job to control others, rather, it's more about allowing love to fuel the freedom we so desire. Love is patient. Love is kind. Love does not envy. Love does not boast. Love is not proud. Love does not dishonor others. Love is not self-seeking. Love is not easily angered. Love keeps no records of wrongs. Love does not delight in evil. Love rejoices with the truth. Love always protects. Love always trusts. Love always hopes. Love always preserves. "When the power of love overcomes the love of power, the world will know peace."

Questions to Ponder:

If the script were to be flipped, how would I want someone to love me and pray for me if I were the "enemy"? Are you embodying the spirit, or are you just "playing God"?

Prayer:

Father, open my heart and mind to fully rest and walk through You. May my resentment dissipate. For we do not dictate each other's fate. May we come as we are and allow Your international love to consume our spirits. May the same love that transforms our spirits also breaks us free from hate and vengeance. May our souls know everlasting peace.

Scripture: Gen 13:8 -Gracious Love

____

____

____

____

____

What do you hear from this scripture? What is God saying to you?

____

____

____

____

____

Reflection/Your Story:

____

____

____

____

____

Activity:

____

____

____

____

____

Questions to Ponder:

____

____

____

____

____

Prayer:

____

____

____

____

____

Scripture: Matthew 22:37-39 – Neighborly Love

Jesus said unto him, 'Thou shalt love the Lord thy God with all thy heart, and with all thy soul, and with all thy mind. This is the first and great commandment. And the second is like unto it, Thou shalt love thy neighbor as thyself.'

What do you hear from this scripture? What is God saying to you?

You need to put him first in life, no matter what. Love God as He loves you. And love each other in the same way.

Reflection/Your Story:

I would like to reflect on just the start of the pandemic how uncertain things were. A lot of people were afraid; I even heard that some people were having anxiety and panic attacks. Everything was so uncertain, it was like something we had never seen or heard of before. A lot of loved ones have died from the virus and some have gotten very sick, but at the end of the day God was with us every step of the way, He said he will never leave us or forsake us and we are still standing and fighting the fight. I, myself, had the virus at the peak of it before the vaccines. I was scared at first, but it was God's love that got me through. God's love is the kind of love that in the midst of any storm, you go through His love and protection will be with you. That's the love He wants for all of us.

Life as we know it is hard, especially these past couple of years. It's been hard on everyone. Being there for each other and caring about others is what will get us through everything.

Activity:

Offering a neighbor, family member, or friend your time, like stating, "If you ever need something, just let me know." Or just checking in from time to time.

Questions to Ponder:

When's the last time you told someone you care about, that you love them?

How often do you check on friends/family?

Prayer:

Dear Heavenly Father, thank you for every day of life. I pray for my family and friends and this whole nation. I pray that we can all come together in Your name. Amen.

Scripture: Gen 13:8 -Gracious Love

What do you hear from this scripture? What is God saying to you?

Reflection/Your Story:

Activity:

Questions to Ponder:

Prayer:

Scripture: John 14:23 – Intimate Love

Jesus replied, "Loving me empowers you to obey my word. And my Father will love you so deeply that we will come to you and make you our dwelling place." TPT

Jesus answered and said to him, "If anyone loves Me, he will keep my word and My Father will love him, and We will come to him and make Our home with him."

What do you hear from this scripture? What is God saying to you?

Love gives power. God's love for us creates our love for Him. His love continues to unfold and revelation pours into us. We turn ourselves to love God. He turns up the fire. It's not weighty, for more from us. Because of who He is and is able to do. God jumps in and creates an atmosphere to empower you. He says, "We will come to Him and make Our home (dwelling) with Him."

Reflection/Your Story:

I had God's revelation flood my soul. I've had difficult hard times in business and marriage, being a mother, and even in turning to God. Then all I may have is a question and they give me my peace and trust with word in my heart, in devotion, through my pastor, or sometimes a TV evangelist, and reading the word. As the word says, "We will come to Him and make our home with Him." It comes in with a deep love for you and it stays and dwells there (Romans 5:1-2).

Activity:

I like finding time with the Lord at the top of my day. It's not always easy, it's worth it! Romans eight always apply no condemnation. When I fail to meet the Lord at the top of the day, He meets me throughout the day as we walk and talk all day. Find you time to get yourself to spend time with our Father daily and press in.

Questions to Ponder:

Will your love ever match His?

His love is what matters when we understand this. This will cause you to love, appreciate, and accept His sacrifices of His Son.

Prayer:

Lord, because of Your deep love for me, I will continue to love You and seek Your face daily. Thank you, Lord, for no guilt, no shame, and no condemnation. In Jesus' name… Amen.

Scripture: Gen 13:8 -Gracious Love

What do you hear from this scripture? What is God saying to you?

Reflection/Your Story:

Activity:

Questions to Ponder:

Prayer:

Scripture: 1 Corinthians 12:12-31 – Unconditional Love

The body of God is made up of many members. No matter if we are Jesus or non-Jesus. One part of the body of Christ is not more valuable than the other part, but the lesser member is to be treated with greater respect. The body needs Apostles, Prophets, Teachers, and those with gifts, but all don't possess these, but all are required to excel in love.

What do you hear from this scripture? What is God saying to you?

No Big Is or little Us. Every part of the physical body is needed, and it is the same with the spiritual body of Christ. All members are important. The whole body is needed to operate properly. All may not have specific callings, but all can excel in love.

Reflection/Your Story:

I have experienced the church putting preachers, pastors, and people of influence on pedestals, which is not Godly and overlooking what they call less spiritual. Children, teenagers, young adults, women, and the poor are not spiritual enough for one reason or another (i.e. cliques, not popular, not wealthy or not well-known, etc…).

Activity:

Bake a cake with all the ingredients.

Bake a cake without one ingredient.

Sew a doll and leave the eyes and one leg.

Try to do a project that needs many to do it and you try to do it on your own.

Questions to Ponder:

Is one member better than another member?

Can we cooperate effectively if one member is missing?

Can we live without a member successfully?

Are we to exhort one member over another?

Is love more important than gifts?

Prayer:

Father, make us aware. We are to include others who are different from us to make up the body of Christ. We can not accomplish the kingdom of God while not allowing others with their gifts to be involved. May we embrace all members of the body of Christ. May we not think of ourselves more highly than we ought to. Thank you that Jesus shed His blood for all who would believe. Help us to love each other unconditionally, in Jesus' name…

Scripture: Gen 13:8 -Gracious Love

What do you hear from this scripture? What is God saying to you?

Reflection/Your Story:

Activity:

____

____

____

____

____

Questions to Ponder:

____

____

____

____

____

Prayer:

____

____

____

____

____

WHAT KIND OF LOVE IS THIS?

I AM LOVE…. Valuable, Called, and Destined for God's Purpose. I establish, re-establish, and confirm my relationship with Christ Jesus.

A woman's guide to a closer relationship with the lover of her soul!

Forward

One of the most important reasons we're here is to know who we are and whose we are. In knowing who and whose we are, we must study the Word. The Word/the Bible set standards and boundaries for our life. In studying comes God's presence. God's presence is what impacts the world that we are to influence.

The word and God's presence brings an unconditional, unfathomable, indescribable love for each and every one of us. It's defined specifically for each individual. Although it's a blanketed love, because each one of us is different, it may look different. God is not a God who has a respecter of persons. His love is perfect and unique.

When we encounter and are filled with God's love, we can do and see and understand things that we could not otherwise do or see or understand. Filled with His love, we can endure pain, quell fear, forgive freely, avoid contention, renew strength, and bless and help others in ways surprising even to us.

His love is not gained by anything we do on our own merit. The Bible states that God loved us while we were still sinners; His love abounds from His infinite goodness and mercy. God's love is steadfast and unchanging.

There is nothing stronger than love — even death. In the darkest of times during your life, love will lift you up and carry you forward. This is the love of the Lord and the love of others around you. "Be kind, compassionate, and forgiving to each other, in the same way God forgave you in Christ."

INDEX

15. Consequential Love
16. Abiding Love
17. Transforming Love
18. Renewed Love
19. Active Love
20. Preserving Love
21. Intentional Love
22. Neighborly Love
23. Intimate Love
24. Obedient Love
25. Unconditional Love

Confession

I am gracious; I am courteous, kind, forgiving, and pleasant. I love; I am with great care; I am appreciative, positive, and respectful. I am purified; I am delivered, cleansed, and free. I am useful; I am helpful, beneficial, worthy, and productive. I am protective; I am safeguarded, shatter-proofed, and covered. I am a peacemaker. I am reconciled, an intercessor, and judge. I am truthful; I am sincere, trustworthy, reliable, and faithful. I am humble; I am submissive and noble.

I am dependable; I am loyal, constant, and stable. I am tough; I am strong, long-lasting, determined, and powerful. I am knowing; I am expressive, purposeful, and willful. I am wise; I am informed, discerning, well-advised, and smart. I am uncorrupt; I am undefiled and guiltless.

I am growing; I am prospering, succeeding, and advancing. I am consequential; I am connected, important, and memorable. I am abiding; I am enduring, constant, and eternal. I am transforming; I am rebuilt, renewed, and stirred up. I am renewed; I am established, affirmed, and restored. I am active; I am lively, involved, and a participant. I am preserving; I am looked after and upkept. I am international; I am existing and all-embracing. I am neighborly; I am warmhearted, good-natured, thoughtful, and unselfish. I am intimate; I am closely familiar, devoted, and deep-seated. I am unconditional; I am not subject to, a respecter of persons, unlimited, and wholehearted. I AM LOVE to God (Yahweh), to others, and myself!!!

Conclusion

This devotion is a shared reflection/journey from twenty-two amazing women. They agreed to share their relationship with the Lord with you.

It has been a journey and a war/fight to get this brilliant idea from the Lord written and published.

Because it was the Lord's idea, I knew He would see it through. He is so faithful like that. I give God all the praise and glory for this devotion. I give a sincere gratitude of thanks to the women who made this possible through willingness and obedience.

www.ingramcontent.com/pod-product-compliance
Lightning Source LLC
Chambersburg PA
CBHW022106050726
47591CB00002B/689

* 9 7 8 1 9 6 8 0 9 2 7 0 2 *